MARION BOYARS PUBLISHERS LTD
24 Lacy Road, London SW15 1NL

www.marionboyars.co.uk

Distributed in Australia and New Zealand by Peribo Pty Ltd
58 Beaumont Road, Kuring-gai, NSW 2080

Printed in 2005
10 9 8 7 6 5 4 3 2 1

A CIP catalogue record for this book is available from the British Library.

ISBN 0-7145-3301-7

Set in Caslon 540 Roman 20/26pt
Printed in China

Tongue Twisters to Tangle Your Tongue

ILLUSTRATED BY REBECCA COBB

MARION BOYARS
CHILDREN'S

How much wood would a woodchuck chuck
if a woodchuck could chuck wood?
He would chuck as much as he could
if a woodchuck could chuck wood.

The big black bug bit the big
black bear but the big black
bear bit the big black bug back!

A tudor who tooted a flute, tried to tutor two tooters to toot. Said the two to their tutor, 'Is it easier to toot than to tutor two tooters to toot?'

Sam's shop stocks short spotted socks.

When Theophilus Thadeus Thistledown, the successful thistle-sifter, was sifting a sieve-full of unsifted thistles, three thousand thistles went through the thick of his thumb. Now, if Theophilus Thadeus Thistledown, the successful thistle-sifter, had three thousand thistles through the thick of his thumb, take care when you sift a sieve-full of unsifted thistles to not get three thousand thistles through the thick of your thumb.

There was a young fisher named Fischer
who fished for a fish in a river.
The fish with a grin
pulled the fisherman in,
now they're fishing the river for Fischer.

Pip's pa Pete popped to the pea patch to pick a peck of peas for the pink pig in the pig-pen.

A noisy noise annoys an oyster.

How many cans can a cannibal nibble if a cannibal can nibble cans?
As many cans as a cannibal can nibble if a cannibal can nibble cans.

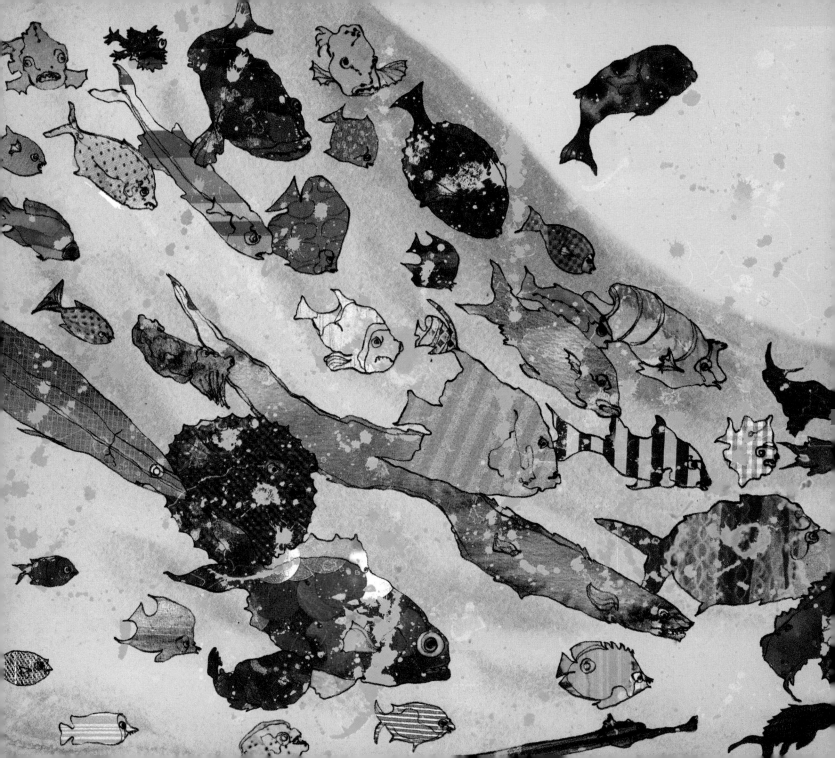

Five frantic frogs fled from fifty fierce fishes.

A moose noshing much mush.

A skunk sat on a stump
and thunk the stump stunk,
but the stump thunk the
skunk stunk too!

A tree toad loved a she-toad
who lived up in a tree.
He was a two-toed tree toad
but a three-toed toad was she.
The two-toed tree toad tried to win
the three-toed she-toad's heart.

For the two-toed tree toad loved the
ground that the three-toed tree toad trod.
But the two-toed tree toad tried in vain
he couldn't please her whim.
From her tree toad bower
with her three-toed power
the she-toad vetoed him.

Pretty Kitty Creighton had a cotton pattern cat,
the cotton pattern cat was bitten by a rat,
the kitten that was bitten had a button for an eye,
and biting off the button made the cotton kitten fly.

Twelve terrible twins twirled twelve tiny twigs.

To begin to toboggan first buy a toboggan.
But do not buy too big a toboggan!
Too big a toboggan is too big a toboggan
to buy to begin to toboggan.

Betty Botter had some butter,
'But,' she said, 'this butter's bitter!
If I bake this bitter butter,
it would make my batter bitter.
But a bit of better butter –
that would make my batter better.'

So she bought a bit of butter,
better than her bitter butter,
and she baked it in her batter,
and the batter was not bitter.
So 'twas better Betty Botter
bought a bit of better butter.

Six slippery snails slid slowly seaward.

Old Oily Ollie oils old oily autos.

Fred fed Ted bread
and Ted fed Fred bread.

Give pop a cup of proper coffee
in a copper coffee cup.

The fat flea flew through
the thin woman's window.

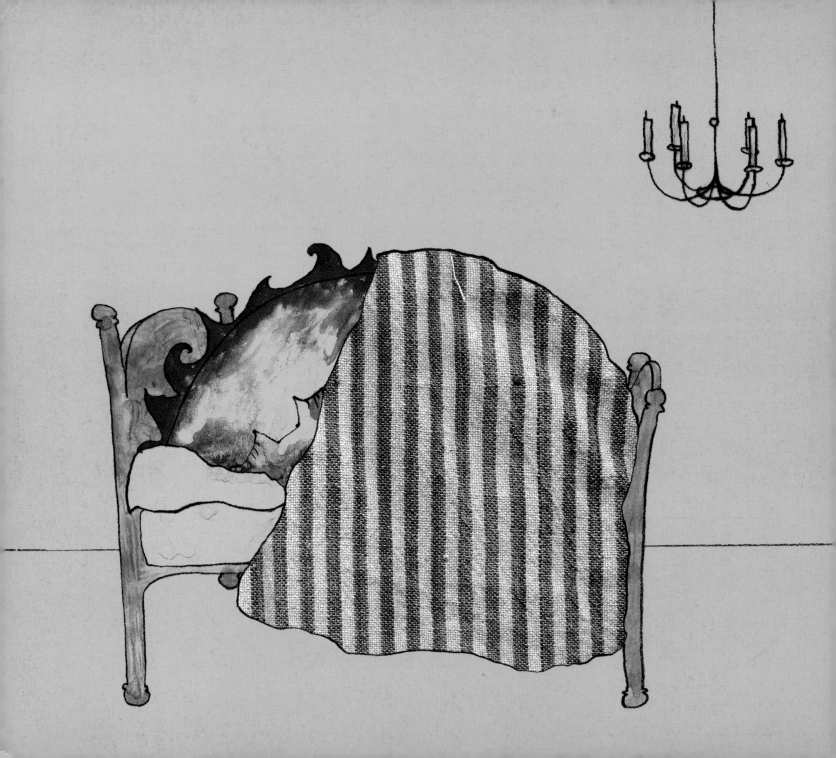

You've no need to light a night-light
on a light night like tonight.
For a night-light's a bright light
and tonight's a night that's light.
When a night's light, like tonight's light
it is really not quite right,
to light night-lights with their bright lights
on a light night like tonight.